Contents

Who was Henry VIII?

Henry VIII was King of England between 1509 and 1547. His family name was Tudor.

The first Tudor

Henry VIII's father, Henry VII, was the first Tudor king.
He won the throne by defeating the previous king, Richard III, at the Battle of Bosworth in 1485. His victory ended the Wars of the Roses, a long struggle for the English throne between two families of nobles – the Yorkists and the Lancastrians. Henry was Lancastrian.

A portrait of Henry VII, Henry VIII's father. He was born in Wales.

 Did you know?

The names of monarchs are often written with Roman numerals after their names. "V" means 5, so "VIII" is 5 + 1 + 1 + 1, which adds up to 8.

4

Disc

WITHDRAWN

WITHDRAWN

Get **more** out of libraries

Please return or renew this item by the last date shown.
You can renew online at www.hants.gov.uk/library
Or by phoning   0845 603 5631

Hampshire
County Council

Moira Butterfield

W
FRANKLIN WATTS

This edition published in 2013 by Franklin Watts

Copyright © Franklin Watts 2013

Franklin Watts
338 Euston Road
London NW1 3BH

Franklin Watts Australia
Level 17/207 Kent Street
Sydney NSW 2000

A CIP catalogue record for this book
is available from the British Library.

Dewey number: 942.05'2'092

ISBN 978 1 4451 1854 3

Printed in China

Franklin Watts is a division of Hachette Children's Books,
an Hachette UK company

www.hachette.co.uk

Designer: Jason Billin
Editor: Sarah Ridley
Art director: Jonathan Hair
Editor-in-Chief: John C. Miles
Picture research: Diana Morris

Key fact

The Lancastrians had a red rose as their badge. The Yorkists had a white rose. Henry VII put them together to make a new badge, the Tudor rose, shown here on a stone carving.

Henry is born

Henry VII married Elizabeth of York, joining the families of York and Lancaster. Elizabeth had two sons, Arthur and Henry. Henry was the younger son, born on 28 June 1491. He grew up in London, in royal palaces dotted around the city. The little prince was looked after by servants and had a life of luxury, but also sadness. He had several sisters and brothers who died young, and his mother died when he was eleven.

A wealthy merchant owned this Tudor bed. Henry would probably have had even grander furniture.

Go and visit

The Merchant's House in Tenby, Pembrokeshire has rooms that look as they did in Tudor times.

Young Henry

Henry's older brother Arthur should have become King, but he died at the age of 16. Henry became the new heir to the throne.

Smart boy

Henry never went to school. Instead he was taught by his own private tutor (teacher). He studied religion, Latin, Greek, music and poetry, and he was said to be clever. He was very religious, too. During his early life the religion in England was Roman Catholic.

Time to marry

Arthur had been married to Catherine of Aragon, the daughter of the King of Spain. When Arthur died, it was arranged that she should marry Henry once he was old enough. Spain was very powerful and the

 Did you know?

Many Tudor people died young because medical treatment was poor.

A painting of Henry as a young man.

English king wanted to have a strong alliance (friendship) with them.

Henry the heart-throb

Henry was a dashing, handsome young prince. He was tall, with red hair, and he loved sports, music and poetry. He was very good at jousting and real tennis – an early type of indoor tennis.

 Key fact

Henry might have grown up to become a Roman Catholic churchman if his brother had not died.

 Go and visit

You can visit Henry's real tennis court at Hampton Court in London, and see people playing.

"Long live the King"

Henry VIII was crowned King at London's Westminster Abbey on 23rd June, 1509, aged 18.

Go and visit

You can visit the site of Henry's coronation at Westminster Abbey in London.

A great party

Henry's father was seen as a grumpy, money-grabbing ruler, so people were pleased to welcome his young, fun-loving son to the throne. They thought that he would lower their taxes and bring happier times. His grand coronation was watched by important nobles and churchmen, and afterwards there was a feast and a jousting tournament.

A new queen

Shortly before he was crowned, Henry married his brother's widow, Catherine of Aragon. There was a religious law against someone marrying their brother's widow, but the

A painting of Henry VIII's coronation.

Pope – the head of the Roman Catholic Church – gave his personal permission for Henry to ignore the rule. Catherine was the daughter of the Spanish King and Queen, Ferdinand and Isabella. When she was just four years old, her parents had agreed that she would marry the future King of England when she grew up.

Key fact

The nobles were the most important families in England. Some of them were related to the royal family.

Did you know?

Catherine of Aragon married Arthur when she was 16, but he died six months later. She married Henry when she was 23. The picture below shows their wedding.

The golden king

The young King Henry was popular, and people thought he was a good ruler.

Henry's court

Wherever Henry went he took his court, a group of nobles and officials. It helped Henry to have the most powerful people in the land near to him, because at court it was difficult for anyone to plot against him and keep it a secret. Courtiers and visitors were kept entertained with lots of events such as tournaments, music and dancing. The King wrote some of the music himself.

Henry's tournament armour at the Royal Armouries in Leeds.

Go and visit

At The Royal Armouries in Leeds you can see this suit of armour made for Henry VIII to wear at tournaments.

Jousting knights were the sports heroes of their day. This painting shows Henry jousting in front of a crowd.

The King at play

Henry thought government duties were boring and preferred to spend the day doing his favourite hobbies. He loved to go hunting on horseback and he flew his own trained birds of prey.

Jousting tournaments

Henry loved jousting, and often held tournaments. He would invite the best jousters to take part, and the court would watch the action from the safety of stands built nearby. Jousting was a dangerous sport, and knights were sometimes injured or killed.

Did you know?

Henry liked to take part in his own tournaments in disguise. He would reveal his true identity at the end.

Foreign friends and enemies

Henry wanted to be seen as a strong military leader, so he went to war against his neighbour, France.

Enemies all around

In Henry's time, Spain, France and the Holy Roman Empire (which included parts of modern-day Germany) were the most powerful countries in Europe, and they were all trying to get as much wealth as they could. Henry wanted the same for England. He fought against France in 1512 and 1513.

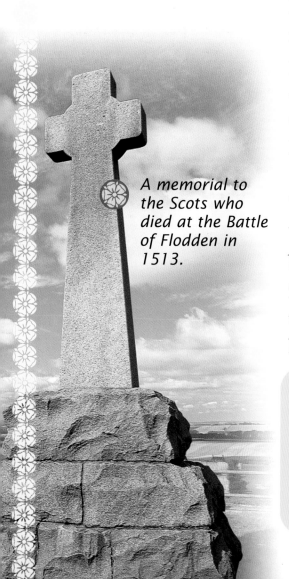

A memorial to the Scots who died at the Battle of Flodden in 1513.

Watch the Scots

While Henry was away in France, his own brother-in-law, James IV of Scotland, invaded England. The Scots were defeated at the Battle of Flodden and 10,000 Scots were killed, including James himself.

 Key fact

Countries often switched alliances during Tudor times. Enemies became friends and friends enemies.

Go and visit

At Branxton in Northumberland you can visit the site of the Battle of Flodden, and walk a battlefield trail to understand what happened during the fighting.

This painting shows Henry VIII arriving at the Field of the Cloth of Gold in France.

Peace and a party

In 1520 Henry sailed across the Channel with his court to meet the French king Francis I to discuss peace. The meeting was held in a huge, luxurious camp called the Field of the Cloth of Gold. There were gold and silver cloth tents for everyone to stay in, and a specially-built gatehouse and fountains.

Did you know?

At the Field of the Cloth of Gold no expense was spared. Tents were lined with pearls and precious gems.

Row with Rome

Henry desperately wanted a son to rule after him. Without one, he thought other nobles might try to take the crown once he died.

Divorce trouble

Catherine and Henry had one surviving child, a daughter called Mary. After nearly 20 years of marriage, Henry decided to divorce Catherine because she was getting too old to have a son, and because he had fallen in love with another woman, Anne Boleyn.

Pope says no

Henry wanted the Pope to "annul" his marriage to Catherine, which meant to declare it had never existed in the first place. Henry now said that because he

 Did you know?

Henry VIII did have a son, called Henry Fitzroy, when he was young. But the baby's mother was not the Queen, so he could not become King.

A portrait of Cardinal Thomas Wolsey, Henry's chief minister.

 Key fact

During this time a German monk called Martin Luther set up a new branch of Christianity called "Protestantism". The spread of the new religion is called the Reformation.

had married his brother's widow, the marriage didn't count in law. Henry's minister Wolsey could not persuade the Pope to agree, so Henry had Wolsey arrested.

Taking charge

Henry appointed two new ministers, Thomas Cromwell and Sir Thomas More. Thomas Cromwell persuaded Henry to make the Church in England break ties with Rome. Once that was arranged, Henry no longer needed the Pope's permission to divorce.

Agree or die

Many English Catholics were very upset by the break with Rome. Sir Thomas More refused to recognise Henry as the head of the new Church of England and, despite being an old friend of Henry's, he was beheaded in 1535.

Hampton Court Palace.

Go and visit

Hampton Court, near London, is a fine palace first built by Wolsey. Henry liked it so much that he made Wolsey give it to him as a present.

Divorce and death

Henry married Anne Boleyn in January 1533, four months before he was officially divorced from his first wife.

Another daughter

Anne was pregnant when she married Henry and she gave birth to a daughter, Elizabeth, in September 1533. Henry had so wanted a son that the birth of Elizabeth was a great disappointment. Eventually she would become one of England's greatest queens, Elizabeth I.

Guilty!

Henry quickly grew tired of Anne and wanted to get rid of her. He accused her of treason, for having love affairs with other men. She was tried, found guilty and executed in the Tower of London in 1536, three years after marrying Henry.

Wedding number three

Henry married a noblewoman, Jane Seymour, two weeks after Anne's execution. In 1537 she gave birth to a

Key fact

Henry accused Anne Boleyn (above) of being unfaithful but the charges were probably untrue. Torture was used to make her so-called lovers admit to whatever Henry wanted.

A view inside the Tower of London. Tower Green is in the centre.

son, Edward, but she died twelve days later. When he was nine Edward eventually became king for a short while after Henry's death, but then he himself died when he was only 16. Henry is said to have been heartbroken by Jane Seymour's death.

Go and visit

Anne Boleyn was kept in prison at the Tower of London, and executed on Tower Green. The spot is marked with a plaque.

The end of the monasteries

Henry had all the Roman Catholic monasteries and convents closed down in England and Wales.

The Dissolution

About 9,000 monks and nuns lived in the monasteries and convents. They followed the orders of the Pope, a link which Henry wanted to destroy. The monasteries also owned valuable farmland, buildings and treasure, which Henry wanted for himself. Henry's minister Thomas Cromwell sent troops to shut the monasteries, and anyone who resisted was imprisoned and sometimes tortured or even executed. The destruction of the monasteries is called the Dissolution.

Modern monks – looking much the same now as in Henry VIII's time.

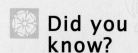

Did you know?

The Abbot (head monk) of Glastonbury Abbey in Somerset resisted the King's men, so he was hanged. Then his head was displayed over the Abbey gates.

A painting of Glastonbury Abbey ruins.

Go and visit

You can visit the ruins of many monasteries that were closed during the Dissolution, for example, Fountains Abbey in Yorkshire and the ruins at Glastonbury Abbey in Somerset (above).

Monastery recycling

Most of the old monasteries were sold off. Some were converted into houses. Others were stripped of their treasures and left to crumble. Stones from the buildings were sometimes taken to build new houses nearby. All the monks and nuns were turned out and given pensions (payments) to live on.

Unpopular people

At the time, monasteries were unpopular with many people and monks were seen as dishonest and badly-behaved. This made it easier for Henry to destroy them.

Key fact

There were about 850 monasteries in England and Wales before the Dissolution. They were all destroyed during the years 1536–40.

Prepared for war

The Pope declared Henry an enemy of the Roman Catholic Church and was willing to help anyone who would overthrow him.

Under threat

It was rumoured that the Catholic Spanish and French kings were raising armies to invade England, with support from the Pope. Henry built forts along the English south coast, in case of an attack from the sea.

Tudor soldiers

Ordinary soldiers in Henry's time did not wear much armour, only a helmet and a breastplate. They were armed with an axe or a

A south coast fort built by Henry to defend England from invasion.

pikestaff, a long wooden pole topped with a spearpoint. Soldiers started to use gunpowder widely, so muskets and pistols began to appear on battlefields.

Henry's navy

Henry ordered new ships to be built for his navy, and his gunmakers made bigger, more powerful cannon than ever before to smash through the sides of enemy ships. The pride of the fleet was the *Mary Rose*, and Henry himself watched it sail from Portsmouth in 1545 to fight an invading French fleet. The French were defeated, but the *Mary Rose* sank before Henry's eyes.

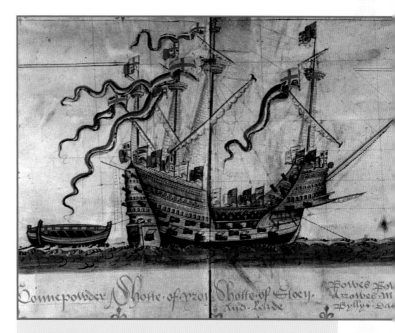

 Key fact

The wreck of the *Mary Rose* (above) was brought up from the seabed in 1982 after over 400 years underwater. An exhibition of the wreck and lots of items from onboard can be seen at Portsmouth Historic Dockyard.

Did you know?

The remains of 200 men and boys were discovered on the wreck of the *Mary Rose*, along with lots of objects, such as clothes and dice.

Married again

England urgently needed other powerful countries to help it against its Catholic enemies.

The best bride

The best way to make an alliance with another country was for Henry to marry a foreign princess. Thomas Cromwell arranged for the King to marry Anne, the sister of a German ruler, the Duke of Cleves. His small country also rejected the Catholic Church.

Six-month marriage

Hans Holbein, Henry's court painter, was sent to paint a portrait of Anne. Henry admired the portrait, and agreed to marry Anne. But Holbein had made her look prettier than she really was. When she arrived Henry thought she was ugly, while she thought he was fat and frightening. The couple married in January 1540 but divorced in July.

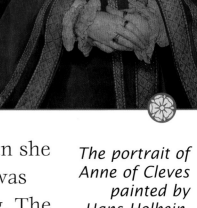

The portrait of Anne of Cleves painted by Hans Holbein.

Did you know?

After her divorce, Anne of Cleves was given the honorary title of "The King's Sister". She carried on living in England, well away from Henry.

Cromwell falls

Henry blamed Thomas Cromwell for his disastrous marriage. Cromwell was arrested and executed (put to death), without even a trial. He had many enemies who hated him for his part in splitting England from the Catholic Church. They did all they could to disgrace him.

 Key fact

By the time of Cromwell's death, Henry's court was no longer a carefree place but was full of distrust and fear. The King was unpredictable and very bad-tempered.

 Go and visit

At the National Portrait Gallery in London, you can come face-to-face with portraits of Henry and some of his wives and ministers.

Portrait of Thomas Cromwell.

23

The grand life

Henry had many royal palaces. He lived in different ones at different times of the year, along with his court.

Food and feasting

Coping with the King and his court was an enormous task, and the royal palaces needed lots of servants. There were huge kitchens that were always busy, as staff cooked the daily meals needed for hundreds of people. The finest foods were served, including wild boar, venison and even peacocks and swans. Wealthy Tudors also loved expensive sweets made from almonds, dried fruit, spices and sugar.

Greenwich Palace, where Henry was born, faced on to the River Thames near London.

 **Go and visit**

Hampton Court has a large Tudor kitchen (left). Meat was cooked on spits in the extra-large fireplaces, which were kept burning constantly.

Key fact

Henry saw his palaces as being symbols of his power, and so he spent a lot of money on them to make them impressive.

Did you know?

Running water was piped into Hampton Court, which was very unusual for the time. Most people had to go and collect water.

Smelly summer

Some of Henry's palaces were located on the River Thames outside London, in small villages such as Greenwich and Hampton (now parts of London). The King and his court would sail by barge to get there. In summer they avoided the centre of the city because hot weather made it smelly and unhealthy.

Fires and furniture

Palaces such as Hampton Court had the very best furniture and decorations. Beautiful tapestries hung on the walls and Henry ordered the very latest modern features, such as chimneys to take away the smoke from every room, and even toilets with running water.

Two more Catherines

Henry married twice more before his death. His fifth wife was executed, but his sixth wife outlived him.

Henry in his later years – a portrait painted in about 1537.

Another bride beheading

Henry's fifth wife was Catherine Howard, the niece of a powerful noble called the Duke of Norfolk. Henry married Catherine in 1540, when she was only 19 and he was 49. She was accused of being unfaithful to the King and was beheaded less than two years after her wedding.

> ### Did you know?
> Catherine Howard asked for the executioner's block to be brought into her room in the Tower of London so she could practise putting her head on it.

Go and visit

Sudeley Castle in Gloucestershire, where Catherine Parr lived after Henry died. She then married Thomas Seymour.

Wife number six

Henry married Catherine Parr, his sixth wife, in 1543. She had no children with Henry, but she encouraged him to take more interest in his daughters, Mary and Elizabeth, and she helped with Prince Edward's education. She cared for Henry, whose health began to get much worse as he got older.

This stained glass window at Sudeley Castle shows Catherine Parr and two of her husbands – Henry VIII and Thomas Seymour.

Key fact

Catherine Howard's uncle, the Duke of Norfolk, was an enemy of Thomas Cromwell. The marriage of his niece to the King helped to destroy Cromwell.

The final years

Henry died at the age of 55 in January 1547.

Smelly king

In his later years Henry was overweight and was said to suffer terrible headaches that made him very irritable. He had poison-filled sores on his legs, which meant he could no longer walk, and he smelled awful.

Dangerous old age

As he aged, Henry became more and more suspicious of anyone who he thought might turn against him. On his orders, lots of people were tortured and executed and, by the end, few people were unhappy at his death. He had begun his reign as a popular and carefree young man but ended it as a violent, unhappy tyrant.

Did you know?

Henry became so suspicious that he locked himself into his bedchamber at night, in case anybody tried to kill him.

A gigantic suit of armour made for Henry in his later years.

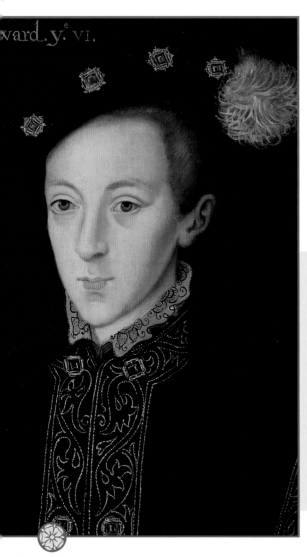

Trouble left behind

Henry's son gained the throne, followed in turn by his two daughters. Henry's break with the Catholic Church caused violence between Roman Catholics and Protestants in England during the reigns of his three children.

Portrait of Henry's son, Edward VI.

Henry's simple tomb in Windsor Castle. He ordered a grand monument, but it was never built.

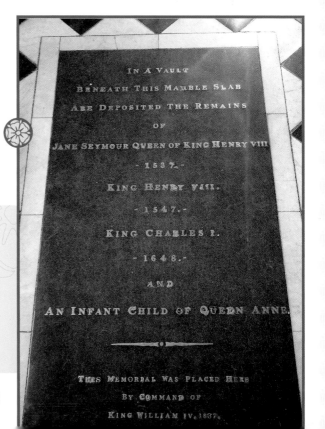

IN A VAULT BENEATH THIS MARBLE SLAB ARE DEPOSITED THE REMAINS OF JANE SEYMOUR QVEEN OF KING HENRY VIII - 1537 - KING HENRY VIII. - 1547 - KING CHARLES I. - 1648 - AND AN INFANT CHILD OF QUEEN ANNE. THIS MEMORIAL WAS PLACED HERE BY COMMAND OF KING WILLIAM IV. 1837.

Glossary

alliance
A friendship between countries, particularly in wartime.

annul
To declare officially that something never counted in the first place, such as Henry's marriage to Catherine of Aragon.

Cardinal
One of the most important positions in the Roman Catholic Church.

Catholic Church
The Christian Church which has the Pope as its head.

coronation
The ceremony when the crown is placed on a new king or queen's head, to mark the official beginning of their reign.

Dissolution, the
The destruction of the monasteries in England and Wales between 1536 and 1540, ordered by Henry VIII.

heir
The next-in-line to the throne, usually the eldest child of the king. Women only become heirs if the monarch has no sons.

jousting
An event in which knights tried to knock each other off their horses with lances.

noble
A member of the most powerful and wealthy families of the country, given titles such as Baron and Lord.

Pope
The head of the Catholic Church, based in Rome.

Protestant Church
A new branch of the Christian Church which was set up in Tudor times, rejecting the rule of the Pope and the beliefs of the Catholic Church.

tax
A sum of money that the people of a country are made to pay to the king's ministers, to raise money for the king to spend.

treason
The crime of plotting against a king or queen.

Tudor
The name of Henry VIII's family. Henry VII, Henry VIII, Edward VI, Mary I and Elizabeth I were all Tudor monarchs.

Tudor Rose
The badge of the Tudor family, which combined a red and a white rose.

Timeline

1485 Henry Tudor is crowned King and the Tudor period begins.

1491 Prince Henry (later Henry VIII) is born at Greenwich Palace.

1502 Prince Arthur dies. Prince Henry becomes heir to the throne.

1509 Henry VII dies. Prince Henry marries Catherine of Aragon and is crowned King Henry VIII.

1516 Princess Mary (later Mary I) is born.

1533 Henry divorces Catherine of Aragon and marries Anne Boleyn.

1533 Princess Elizabeth (later Elizabeth I) is born.

1533-34 The English Church becomes independent of Rome.

1536 Henry has Anne Boleyn executed for treason. He marries Jane Seymour. The Dissolution of the Monasteries begins.

1537 Prince Edward (later Edward VI) is born and Jane Seymour dies.

1540 Henry marries and divorces Anne of Cleves. Thomas Cromwell is executed. Henry marries Catherine Howard.

1542 Catherine Howard is executed.

1543 Henry marries Catherine Parr.

1545 The *Mary Rose* sinks.

1547 Death of Henry VIII.

Websites

www.royalarmouries.org
Find out about the Tudor weapons and armour at the National Museum of Arms and Armour.

www.maryrose.org
Find out about the *Mary Rose* exhibition. Take a virtual tour of the ship and meet the crew.

www.hrp.org.uk
The official site of both the Tower of London and Hampton Court. Click on the links to choose which one you'd like to find out about.

www.nationaltrust.org.uk
Find out about Tudor places to visit near you.

www.royalpaperdolls.com
Print off paper dolls of Henry and his wives, and find out all about them.

Index